❧ LAMBS ❧

To Joey
Because he likes animals
From the Dickersons
With all our love

ALFRED A. KNOPF

NEW YORK

BY MARTIN & VIRGINIA WEAVER

LAMBS

❧ FOR JASON & CECILIA ❧

Little Lamb, who made thee?

Dost thou know who made thee?

Gave thee life, and bid thee feed

By the stream and o'er the mead;

Gave thee clothing of delight,

Softest clothing, woolly, bright;

Gave thee such a tender voice,

Making all the vales rejoice?

Little Lamb, who made thee?

Dost thou know who made thee?

–William Blake

The long winter is past. The days are growing warm and bright and the sun has melted the snow from the fields. New blades of green grass are peeping out of the dark ground. It is spring. On farms, mother sheep are beginning to give birth to their lambs in the grassy fields.

Weak and helpless, their eyes shut tight, the wet lambs lie curled up in the grass. Their mothers lick their woolly coats until they are clean and dry. Each mother can tell her baby from all the other lambs by his smell.

෩ Soon the tiny lambs open their eyes and stretch out their limbs. Before long they are standing on wobbly legs, calling out to their mothers in loud, plaintive bleats and looking out at the new world around them.ॐ

From the day they are born, hungry lambs love to drink their mothers' warm milk.

A mother's warm body is a nice place for a cold or tired lamb to cuddle. The woolly babies stay by their mothers' sides, and follow closely after them wherever they go.

The soft fleece of a young lamb, heavy with oil, soon becomes a thick waterproof coat. Even in the rain, the curly wool keeps him cosy and dry.

◄§ Later in the spring, the growing lambs become bolder and begin to wander away from their mothers to explore the pasture. But mother sheep like to keep their lambs nearby, and come to find them if they stay away too long. §►

⋑ As they watch their mothers grazing in the fields, lambs soon discover that grass and other green shoots are good to eat. The more grass they eat, the less they need to drink their mothers' milk. By late spring, most of them are fully weaned. ⋐

When they are big enough to reach the trough, lambs will learn to eat feed and grain.

Day by day the lambs grow more like their mothers. There are black sheep, white sheep and spotted sheep. Some are white with black faces. Some have short, curly wool and others have long, shaggy hair.

Lambs love to frisk and run about in the spring sunshine. They leap and frolic in the grass, bleating wildly and tearing off in short, zig-zag dashes across the pasture.

All through the spring, lambs are learning new things. They learn to stay with the flock. They learn what foods are good to eat and how to find a snug place to rest for the night, sheltered from the chilly winds.

Summer has come. The lambs have grown into young sheep. Next year, in the early springtime, new lambs will be born in these same fields.

eς WITH THANKS TO FARMERS PATERSON & TIPPLES ϶ε

without whose lambs this book would not have been possible.

Text set in Linofilm Palatino
Composed by Volk & Huxley, Inc., New York, New York
Printed by Rae Publishing Co., Cedar Grove, New Jersey
Bound by Economy Bookbinding Corp., Kearny, New Jersey
Typography by Thomas Morley